I0409014

1

Contents

Preface

Today's business world is facing ever-changing dynamics and competitive conditions like never before. It's undeniable that technical skills are crucial, but equally important is another factor: interpersonal relationships and leadership skills. This is precisely where the concepts of leadership and human relations come to the forefront in the business world.

This book has been prepared to address leadership and human relations, explaining how these two fundamental elements can be better understood and effectively managed in the business world. Leadership doesn't only mean being the CEO of a company or the manager of a department; leadership is a critical skill for everyone at every level and in every position. These leadership skills play a significant role not only in the business world but also in your personal life.

What Will You Find in This Book?

Our book explores the concepts that form the foundation of leadership and human relations. You will discover different leadership models in the business world and explore the advantages of these models. You will understand the importance of effective communication strategies and workplace communication. Additionally, you will learn ways to strengthen your interpersonal relationships and critical concepts such as mentorship. The book also delves into conflict management and leadership during moments of crisis. We will examine how to adapt to future trends in leadership and human relations in the business world.

This book provides valuable information for both beginners in the fields of leadership and human relations and experienced professionals. We aim to provide you with tools and insights that will help you understand the complexity of the business world and improve your ability to build better relationships with people.

In each chapter of the book, you will find real-world examples and practical tips. Furthermore, we offer thought-provoking questions and exercises to help you enhance your skills in leadership and human relations.

Let's Get Started!

This book is an invitation to embark on a journey into the realms of leadership and human relations in the business world. We invite you to take the first steps towards becoming a better leader and strengthening your interpersonal relationships. Are you ready? If so, we recommend setting aside a few hours to begin this exciting journey into the world of leadership and human relations in the business world.

With warm regards,

Haktan AYDIN

Introduction

Purpose of the Book

This book aims to address the topics of leadership and human relations in the business world, emphasizing how crucial these two critical elements are in professional life. Leadership in the business world is not just a position; it reflects a mindset and an approach. Leadership is the characteristic that successfully guides an organization's goals and propels its team forward. This book presents leadership as a skill that can be developed by individuals at every level and in every position, not just top-level executives.

Simultaneously, human relations are a foundational cornerstone in the business world. Good relationships enhance collaboration, improve communication, and boost employee motivation. This book underscores the importance of skills such as effective communication, empathy, teamwork, and conflict management by examining the critical role of human relations in achieving success at work. The knowledge about human relations is essential for every business professional to excel in their career.

This book aspires to provide the tools necessary for success in both leadership and human relations in the business world. It emphasizes that professionals at all levels in the business world must enhance their leadership and human relations skills to advance their careers and add value to their organizations. With real-world examples, practical applications, and guidance, this book aims to help readers maximize their potential in their careers.

The Importance of Leadership and Human Relations in the Business World

The business world is filled with constantly changing dynamics and rapidly evolving technology. Today's work environment goes beyond success based solely on technical skills. In the process of carrying out our work, our relationships with people, our communication skills, and our leadership abilities are of great significance. Therefore, the concepts of leadership and human relations have become keys to success in the business world.

Leadership does not concern only company presidents or top-level managers; it affects every employee at every level and in every position. This book explains that leadership skills hold universal importance and have a significant impact not only in the business world but also in personal life. Leadership is more than just the skill to manage a team; it is the art of instilling an influential vision in the hearts of followers, maximizing people's potential, and providing the strength and flexibility required to overcome challenges.

Additionally, success in the business world is determined not only by an individual's technical abilities but also by the relationships they build with others. Effective communication and positive relationships among individuals are fundamental for an organization's success. This book underscores how critical human relationships are in the business world and highlights the importance of developing and maintaining these relationships.

Successful leaders are individuals who not only possess managerial skills but also have the ability to motivate, support, and empower people. This book aims to support the journey of those who have embarked on developing their leadership skills by presenting leadership principles and practices.

Furthermore, leadership and human relations skills are not limited to the business world; they are also highly valuable in personal life. Building strong relationships, effective communication, and adapting leadership skills to personal life can lead to a more fulfilling and balanced life.

This book, by covering both leadership and human relations topics, aims to provide readers with the tools necessary to succeed in the business world and personal life. It is designed as a resource for anyone who wishes to delve deep into the subjects of leadership and human relations, helping them understand the complexities of the business world and enhance their ability to build strong relationships with people. We are here to guide you throughout the book. Now, let's begin our journey into the realms of leadership and human relations in the business world!

Structure of the Book

This book, by addressing leadership and human relations in the business world, aims to emphasize the critical importance of these two elements in professional and personal development.

Understanding the Foundations: In the first section, we will lay the groundwork for the concepts of leadership and human relations. We will explain why leadership and human relations are so important and examine the fundamental principles that will help us understand the roles of these two subjects in the business world and our personal lives. We will also explain how this book can benefit you.

Leadership Models and Advantages: In the second section, we will explore different leadership models used in the business world. We will delve into each leadership model in detail and discuss the advantages that will help you understand which model is more effective in various situations. This section will assist you in determining and improving your leadership style.

Effective Communication and the Importance of Workplace Communication: In the third section, we will discover that communication is the cornerstone of leadership and human relations. We will examine effective communication strategies and emphasize the importance of workplace communication. By enhancing your communication skills, you will become a more effective communicator both in the business world and in your personal life.

Strengthening Human Relations: In the fourth section, we will address the critical role of strengthening human relations. While examining concepts such as mentorship, collaboration, and teamwork, you will learn how to build solid relationships with others. This section will help you enhance your ability to understand people and work better with them.

Conflict Management and Leadership in Times of Crisis: In the fifth section, you will learn how to manage conflicts in the business world and how to exercise leadership during moments of crisis. By developing conflict resolution skills, you will learn how to turn negative situations into positive outcomes and deal with crises effectively.

The Future of Leadership and Human Relations: In the sixth and final section, you will explore how to adapt to the ever-changing nature of the business world and discover future trends in leadership and human relations. You will learn how to compete in a changing business environment and carry your leadership skills into the future.

Each chapter will include real-world examples and practical tips. Additionally, we will provide thought-provoking questions and exercises to help you improve your leadership and human relations skills. This book is designed as a resource for anyone who wishes to delve deep into the subjects of leadership and human relations and aims to help you embark on a more effective, satisfying, and successful journey in both the business world and personal life.

What is Leadership and Human Relations?

Concept of Leadership

Leadership is the process of guiding others, either an individual or a group of people, towards a goal or vision. However, leadership is not confined to a position or a title; it is also a manner of behavior, a lifestyle, and an approach. Leadership goes beyond giving orders or making decisions; it involves inspiring, motivating, nurturing development, and encouraging individuals to strive for excellence.

Being a good leader means valuing not only your own success but also the success of your team and the people around you. Leadership requires the ability to focus on collective goals rather than individual interests. Leaders strive to understand the potential of each team member and help them maximize it. Additionally, leaders guide, support, and mentor team members to recognize their strengths and improve their weaknesses.

Leadership also entails having a vision. A good leader possesses the ability to foresee the future and guides everyone towards the same goal by sharing that vision with the team. A leader exhibits an inspiring energy to progress towards the goal even in the face of challenges. Furthermore, leadership involves communication skills. A good leader can communicate openly, show empathy, and understand people's emotions to motivate them effectively.

Leadership also involves fostering collaboration and teamwork, in addition to having an influential and powerful leadership style. Leaders bring together individuals with different talents and perspectives, allowing everyone to showcase their strengths. This enhances both individual and team success.

Leadership is not just about overcoming a position; it encompasses guiding, inspiring, motivating, and leading the process of achieving common goals. A good leader sees the potential in people and offers the guidance needed to lead them towards a better future.

Meaning of Human Relations

Human relations are a fundamental component of leadership and are considered the key to success in both the business world and personal life. Here is more information on how human relations impact leadership and success:

Human relations essentially refer to the interactions and connections between individuals. These connections are based on emotional bonds such as trust, respect, understanding, and empathy. Strong human relations are built on these core values and reflect how an individual interacts with others.

In the business world, human relations are incredibly important. Succeeding in the workplace is not just about possessing technical skills; it also requires the ability to communicate effectively and collaborate with others. Strong human relations in the workplace enable employees to collaborate better within their teams and work more efficiently.

There is a close relationship between leadership and human relations. A good leader builds strong relationships with their team and motivates people. Leadership goes beyond giving orders; it involves understanding the emotional needs of your team and guiding them. A good leader values both individual and collective success within the team and encourages it.

Strong human relations in the workplace can enhance collaboration and productivity. When you have a solid relationship with your colleagues and supervisors, you can communicate better and collaborate more effectively. This leads to faster project completion and increased efficiency in the workplace.

Leadership and human relations are integral to success in both the business world and personal life. A good leader establishes strong human relationships and motivates their team, while every employee at all levels should have the ability to collaborate. Trust, respect, and understanding form the foundation of successful human relations and are critical for both leadership and personal success.

The Relationship Between Leadership and Human Relations

Undoubtedly, the relationship between leadership and human relations is quite intricate and mutually reinforcing. Both fields can positively influence each other, ultimately enhancing success. Here is a deeper analysis of this relationship:

A good leader establishes strong human relations. This means that leaders build a solid, trust-based relationship with their team or team members. When team members trust their leaders, they better understand their leader's vision and put in more effort to realize that vision. Trust enables team members to accompany their leader on the journey of leadership.

Leadership encompasses guiding and motivating the team. A good leader listens to team members, considers their concerns and suggestions, and is responsive to their needs. This is a reflection of the power of human relations. When team members feel understood by their leaders, they feel a stronger sense of commitment and respect towards their leadership.

Possessing good human relations skills can amplify a leader's impact. Human relations involve personal and emotional connections, allowing leaders to communicate on a deeper level with their team members. When team members feel valued and cared for by their leaders, they become more motivated to work.

Moreover, in a workplace where leaders establish good human relations, collaboration and teamwork become more efficient. Strong relationships among colleagues mean better communication and more effective solution-oriented work. This contributes to the successful completion of projects and enhances workplace efficiency.

Leadership and human relations are two significant components that feed into each other. A good leader gains the trust of their team by forming strong human relationships and assists them in achieving their vision. Similarly, a workplace with strong human relations fosters collaboration and teamwork, encouraging success. This mutual relationship between leadership and human relations is of critical importance in both the business world and personal life.

Leadership Models in the Business World

Transformational Leadership

Certainly, transformational leadership is an influential leadership model that aims to guide team members towards a pioneering vision. These leaders adopt an inspirational approach to maximize the potential of team members and encourage them for personal and professional development.

The key characteristics of transformational leaders may include:

Having a Vision: Transformational leadership begins with a leader having a clear and inspiring vision. This vision includes the goals and objectives that the leader will guide the team toward. For example, a business leader may carry a vision of ensuring the sustainability and growth of the company in the future. This vision serves as a focal point that unites the efforts of the leader and the team.

Inspiration and Motivation: Transformational leaders motivate their team members by conveying their visions

Moreover, in a workplace where leaders establish good human relations, collaboration and teamwork become more efficient. Strong relationships among colleagues mean better communication and more effective solution-oriented work. This contributes to the successful completion of projects and enhances workplace efficiency.

Leadership and human relations are two significant components that feed into each other. A good leader gains the trust of their team by forming strong human relationships and assists them in achieving their vision. Similarly, a workplace with strong human relations fosters collaboration and teamwork, encouraging success. This mutual relationship between leadership and human relations is of critical importance in both the business world and personal life.

and understanding communication. Regular communication with team members, listening to their thoughts and feelings, forms the foundation of strong and reliable relationships.

Leading by Example: Transformational leaders represent themselves as examples through their leadership. They demonstrate the desired behaviors and adhere to their values and ethical standards to inspire others. This helps leaders create a trustworthy and powerful impact.

Transformational leadership can be a powerful tool to promote success in both the business world and personal life. These leaders effectively lead by unleashing the potential of team members, promoting change, and inspiring with a visionary approach. This model can contribute to the growth of organizations and individuals.

Ethical Leadership

Ethical leadership is an approach where leaders focus on making decisions based on ethical and moral values. These leaders consider values such as honesty, fairness, respect, and responsibility as fundamental, guiding businesses and organizations to operate in line with ethical standards and societal values.

These leaders inspire team members by setting examples. They concretely reflect ethical values through their actions, motivating team members to adhere to these values. Especially in challenging decision-making moments, ethical leaders emphasize the importance of ethical values and strive to make decisions that align with them.

Ethical leadership is critical for the sustainability and reputation of organizations. This leadership approach boosts employee morale, increases internal motivation, and promotes collaboration. Additionally, it helps organizations establish a more positive image within society. Customers, suppliers, and other stakeholders are more satisfied working with an organization that adheres to ethical values, providing a critical advantage for long-term success.

Ethical leadership is an approach where leaders consider more than just financial success. These leaders guide organizations to operate in line with ethical values, aiming not only for short-term gains but also for long-term sustainability and societal impact. In this way, they contribute to a better future, both within the organization and in the broader community.

Autocratic Leadership

Autocratic leadership is a leadership style in which the leader has nearly complete authority over the decision-making process. These leaders often limit or entirely eliminate the participation of team members in decision-making and make decisions on their own. Autocratic leaders can make quick decisions and effectively manage urgent situations, but this leadership style has significant disadvantages in the long term.

Autocratic leaders can restrict the motivation and creativity of team members due to the intense control in the decision-making process. Team members may lose their commitment to their work because of limited or no participation. This can weaken emotional connections between employees and the organization, hindering their loyalty. Moreover, it may hinder team members from fully utilizing their potential and make it difficult to come up with creative solutions.

In the long run, autocratic leadership can lead to communication problems within the organization. Because leaders make decisions on their own without hearing the ideas or concerns of team members, the desire of team members to communicate with their leaders may decrease. Consequently, communication within the organization can deteriorate, and a lack of collaboration can arise.

However, autocratic leadership can be necessary in certain situations. It can be effective when quick decisions are needed, or when the leader possesses superior knowledge and experience compared to others. Nevertheless, in general, long-term success may require the adoption of more participatory and democratic leadership styles. These leadership approaches increase motivation, stimulate creativity, and create a more robust communication environment within the organization.

Distributed Leadership

Distributed leadership is an approach that goes beyond traditional leadership models, aiming to distribute leadership responsibilities not to one individual but among a group or many members of an organization. In this model, leadership responsibilities are shared collectively rather than being concentrated in one leader. This can help organizations manage more effectively and flexibly.

Distributed leadership encourages the combining of various skills and expertise within the organization. This approach allows leadership tasks to be allocated to the most suitable individuals in different areas. For example, one person with the best technical knowledge might take the leadership role in managing the technical aspects of a project, while others may lead in areas like project communication or team motivation.

Distributed leadership emphasizes collaboration and communication within the organization. It promotes a more participatory and democratic environment rather than a hierarchical one. When collaboration and knowledge sharing are encouraged, there is a higher likelihood of better ideas emerging and creative problem-solving.

However, distributed leadership requires effective communication and coordination within the organization. Sharing leadership responsibilities necessitates good communication and teamwork. Furthermore, providing training and development opportunities for everyone to take on leadership roles is essential.

Distributed leadership can help organizations manage more flexibly and diversely. This leadership approach enables individuals within the organization to realize their potential and share leadership responsibilities collectively. However, effective implementation may require good communication, collaboration, and coordination.

Charismatic Leadership

Charismatic leadership is a leadership model characterized by the leader's personal charm, charisma, and inspirational qualities. These leaders not only hold influence due to their positions but also due to the powerful impact of their personal traits. Charismatic leaders bring team members together around an inspiring vision and motivate them in an inspiring way.

These leaders can build a strong connection between themselves and their team members, encouraging team members to identify with them. Team members take pride in working with charismatic leaders and see their successes as their own. This motivates team members to be committed to the leader's goals and puts in extra effort.

Charismatic leaders are often strong in decision-making and providing inspiration. Their visionary thinking combines with determination. These leaders motivate team members to deal with uncertainty or challenging situations and emphasize the importance of working together to overcome such situations.

However, the charismatic leadership model has some potential challenges. Primarily, because it relies heavily on the leader's personal charisma, changes or replacements in leadership can lead to uncertainty and a loss of commitment within the organization. Additionally, charismatic leaders may sometimes make emotionally driven decisions, which can lead them away from logical and data-driven decision-making.

Charismatic leadership is defined by the leader's personal appeal and inspiring qualities. These leaders bring team members together around a vision and inspire them. However, the sustainability and impact of this leadership style may depend on the leader's individual charisma and can create uncertainties with leadership changes.

The Role of Human Relationships in the Business World

The Importance of Interpersonal Relationships in the Workplace

Undoubtedly, the role of interpersonal relationships in the business world is a critical reality. Interpersonal relationships in the workplace are a fundamental factor that significantly influences the success and productivity of an organization. These relationships shape the atmosphere of the workplace and make substantial contributions to the overall health of the organization.

Strong interpersonal relationships in the workplace are one of the cornerstones of an organization. The business world is complex, requiring people with diverse skills, experiences, and perspectives to work together. Good interpersonal relationships help establish trust among team members. This trust is a fundamental requirement for collaboration and open communication. Without collaboration, organizations cannot operate efficiently and achieve their goals. Good interpersonal relationships foster this collaboration and enable team members to work more effectively by trusting each other.

Furthermore, strong interpersonal relationships in the workplace can enhance employee job satisfaction. Satisfied employees are more committed to their work and perform at a higher level. Good interpersonal relationships increase employees' commitment to their jobs and the organization, potentially reducing turnover rates and helping the organization retain talented personnel.

Additionally, solid interpersonal relationships can reduce stress in the workplace. Positive workplace relationships help employees feel safe and better equipped to cope with work-related stress. This can contribute to a decrease in health issues and work-related stress.

In the business world, strong interpersonal relationships are a fundamental element for the success of organizations and the happiness of employees. These relationships build trust, respect, and collaboration, increase workplace satisfaction, and make employees happier and more motivated. Therefore, business leaders and managers should pay attention to interpersonal relationships and encourage employees to build strong connections with each other and the organization.

The Impact of Interpersonal Relationships on Work Performance

Interpersonal relationships create a strategic advantage in the business world. Employees work alongside individuals with different skills, experiences, and perspectives. Good interpersonal relationships facilitate communication among these differences and create a collaborative environment. Collaboration helps complete projects more effectively and efficiently. Team members understand each other better, solve problems more quickly, and engage in more effective knowledge sharing.

Strong interpersonal relationships can also boost employee motivation. People feel more inclined to work in an environment where they get along, respect each other, and receive support. Positive relationships help employees become more motivated because coming to work becomes a more enjoyable experience.

Positive relationships among colleagues can make work more enjoyable for employees. A good working relationship with colleagues can make employees look forward to coming to work and cooperating. This can help balance the more challenging aspects of the job and sustain motivation.

Additionally, strong interpersonal relationships contribute to employees developing an emotional attachment to their work. Positive relationships among colleagues and leaders can lead employees to feel loyal to the organization and more committed to its goals. This can result in employees investing more energy and effort into their work.

Leaders and managers being empathetic and supportive of their employees increase motivation and commitment levels. Empathetic leadership helps employees understand their emotional needs and feel valued. Supportive leaders assist employees in coping with difficulties and realizing their potential, which, in turn, increases motivation.

In the business world, interpersonal relationships are a fundamental source of motivation. Positive and supportive relationships help employees become more committed to their jobs, more motivated, and higher-performing. Good relationships can make employees look forward to coming to work and can boost the positive energy in the workplace. Therefore, organizations should create an empathetic and supportive work environment, and leaders should make an effort to understand and support the emotional needs of their employees.

Leadership Skills and Qualities

Definition of Leadership Skills

Leadership skills help a leader guide an organization or team towards its goals. Leaders must convey their vision while charting the course for the organization. A good leader can clearly articulate this vision and rally team members around it. This facilitates progress toward common goals and motivates team members.

Leadership skills also encompass effective communication. Leaders share information, give instructions, and receive feedback by communicating openly and effectively with team members. Good communication encourages collaboration, reduces misunderstandings, and builds a strong communication network within the organization.

Leadership requires decision-making skills. Leaders often face complex problems and must make the right decisions that can shape the organization's future. Good leaders analyze information, assess risks, and make the right decisions in a timely manner.

Problem-solving abilities are also a crucial part of leadership skills. Leaders must find creative and effective solutions to the challenges that their organization or team faces. This supports the sustainability and growth of the organization.

Lastly, leadership skills involve maximizing the potential of team members. Good leaders guide team members, provide development opportunities, and motivate them. This helps the organization make the most efficient use of its human resources.

Leadership skills are fundamental abilities that significantly influence a leader's success and the organization's goals. Skills like conveying a vision, effective communication, decision-making, problem-solving, and fostering team member development shape a leader's success and the organization's goals. Therefore, leaders must strive to develop and apply these skills critically.

Leadership Qualities

Undoubtedly, leadership is a complex concept that involves more than just skills and requires specific qualities beyond being a good leader. Leadership finds its true meaning through the amalgamation of these qualities.

A good leader paints a rich profile in terms of leadership qualities. These qualities shape the leader's personality and leadership style, increasing their impact on team members. The most important qualities among these are honesty and respect. An honest leader shares information through open communication and creates a trustworthy environment. A respectful leader values the opinions and feelings of team members, fostering positive collaboration and workplace relationships.

Moreover, leaders must possess the quality of determination. Determined leaders focus on goals, do not give up in the face of challenges, and motivate team members. This quality demonstrates a leader's ability to deal with difficult situations and inspires team members.

Empathy is another crucial quality in leadership. An empathetic leader understands the needs and emotional states of team members. This enables the leader to adopt a human-centered approach and helps in building a stronger bond with team members.

A sense of justice is another leadership quality. A just leader makes decisions based on the principles of equality and objectivity. This ensures that team members trust the leader's decisions and contributes to the creation of a fair work environment.

Effective communication skills are also indispensable qualities for a leader. Leaders motivate team members by effectively conveying their visions and goals. Good communication enables the leader to deliver their message clearly and comprehensibly.

Leaders with these qualities earn the trust of team members and can use their leadership more effectively. However, it's important to remember that leadership qualities are qualities that can be developed and reinforced. Leaders must continuously work on self-improvement, remain open to feedback, and integrate these qualities into their daily leadership practices.

Leadership qualities, just like leadership skills, assist a leader in guiding effectively. Honesty, respect, determination, empathy, a sense of justice, and effective communication skills allow a leader to set an example for team members and support the organization's success.

Strategies for Developing Leadership Skills

Undoubtedly, leadership skills are qualities that can be developed and continuously reinforced. Leaders should consider various strategies and methods to maximize their leadership potential and develop effective leadership skills.

Education is an important strategy for leaders to improve their leadership skills. Leaders can continuously educate themselves by staying updated on developments in the field of leadership. Leadership training can provide them with new perspectives, teach leadership models, and help improve their communication skills.

Gaining experience is also critical for developing leadership skills. Leaders can gain leadership experience by managing different projects or taking on various responsibilities. These experiences help leaders enhance their problem-solving abilities, their ability to guide team members, and their skills in making strategic decisions.

Receiving feedback is an effective way for leaders to support their development. Leaders can identify their weaknesses and improve them by considering feedback from team members, peers, or upper management. Positive feedback reinforces leaders' strengths and boosts their self-confidence.

Remaining open to learning signifies a leader's willingness to continuously acquire new knowledge and perspectives. Given changing business conditions and leadership approaches, leaders must be flexible and committed to lifelong learning. This strengthens leaders' adaptability.

Mentorship is a way for leaders to receive guidance and counseling from more experienced leaders. A mentor plays a guiding role in a leader's career journey, shares experiences, and helps improve leadership skills. Mentorship relationships can accelerate leaders' learning and help them develop more rapidly.

Leadership skills can be developed and reinforced. By using strategies such as education, gaining experience, receiving feedback, remaining open to learning, and mentorship, leaders can maximize their leadership potential. A good leader focuses on continuous improvement, which enhances not only their personal achievements but also the organization's success.

Communication and Its Role in the Business World

Fundamentals of Effective Communication

Effective communication in the business world is a fundamental element for success. Good communication enables leaders, employees, customers, and other stakeholders to come together, interact, and collaborate.

Effective communication plays a critical role within organizations and between organizations. Within an organization, leaders and managers can convey their visions by establishing accurate and open communication with team members. This communication provides guidance among employees to understand the organization's goals and strategies.

Furthermore, good communication shapes the interaction of organizations with the external world. Effective communication with customers, suppliers, competitors, and other business partners increases collaboration opportunities, aids in problem-solving, and strengthens business relationships.

Clear and open communication ensures that ideas, information, and expectations are expressed clearly. This helps everyone within the organization be on the same page and aligned in the same direction to achieve goals. It reduces misunderstandings and confusion, preventing waste of time and resources.

Effective communication also enhances collaboration and productivity. A good communication environment allows team members to collaborate more effectively and resolve issues more quickly. It can also motivate employees as they feel better understood and valued.

Effective communication is the cornerstone of the business world. It is the key to successful collaboration and effective operations both within and outside organizations. Therefore, it should be acknowledged that leaders, employees, and other stakeholders must focus on improving their effective communication skills as an essential way to enhance organizational success and gain a sustainable competitive advantage.

The Role of Communication in the Business World

Communication plays a vital role at every level in the business world and is a fundamental determinant of organizational success. Communication enables leaders, employees, customers, and other stakeholders to interact within organizations and across organizations.

Communication is a key tool for leaders to convey their organizational visions and strategies. A good leader provides a clear roadmap for collaboration and goals and motivates by communicating this vision to team members. Good communication facilitates understanding among employees and helps them identify with their leaders.

Moreover, communication among employees facilitates the sharing of information and issues. Collaboration and knowledge sharing enhance organizational efficiency and contribute to the early detection and resolution of problems. A culture of transparent communication encourages employees to approach problems more openly and offer solutions.

A good communication culture boosts motivation within the organization. Employees are happier and more motivated in an environment where they feel understood and valued. Effective communication helps employees demonstrate more commitment to their leaders and organizations.

Effective communication also plays a crucial role in strengthening customer relations. Clear and effective communication with customers increases satisfaction and loyalty. Good communication is necessary for receiving customer feedback and responding to customer demands promptly.

Effective communication with the external world positively impacts an organization's reputation. Good communication can clearly convey an organization's values and purposes to its stakeholders. It also enhances the sustainability and competitive advantage of the organization.

Communication is essential in the business world. It serves as a tool for leaders to convey their visions, for employees to share information and issues, and for organizations to strengthen collaboration and operations. A culture of effective communication encourages transparency, boosts motivation, and focuses on organizational goals. Additionally, it is necessary for strengthening customer relations and effectively communicating with the external world. Communication should be recognized as an indispensable element for success in the business world, and organizations should promote and develop effective communication skills.

Communication Challenges and Solutions in the Workplace

While communication is essential in the business world, it is also an inevitable fact that communication challenges exist. The complexity and diversity of the business world can sometimes hinder communication. These challenges may include different perspectives, communication gaps, language barriers, technological obstacles, and more. However, it is possible to overcome these challenges, and a good leader can develop the right strategies and approaches to do so.

Differing perspectives are a common challenge in communication within organizations or between organizations. Different departments or groups may have different viewpoints and priorities. These differences can lead to disagreements and misunderstandings in communication. A good leader can bring different perspectives together, encourage the exchange of ideas, and make efforts to create a common understanding.

Communication gaps can also hinder effective communication. Communication breakdowns or unclear instructions can lead to misdirection and a lack of collaboration. A good leader can establish communication protocols and guidelines to ensure communication is clear and transparent. Additionally, they can use communication channels like regular meetings and feedback processes effectively.

Language barriers are a prevalent communication challenge in today's globalized business world. Communication barriers can arise when people from different cultures communicate. A good leader may have the ability to communicate in various languages or can facilitate communication by using translation services.

Technological obstacles, especially when dealing with remote work or team members in different geographic locations, can create communication challenges. Errors or deficiencies in the use of technology can lead to interruptions or disruptions in communication. A good leader can overcome these obstacles by selecting the right communication tools and providing technology training to the team members.

Communication challenges are inevitable in the business world, but they are obstacles that a good leader can overcome with the right strategies and approaches. Approaches such as bringing different perspectives together, establishing communication protocols, overcoming language barriers, and effectively using communication tools can help leaders support effective communication. A good leader can turn communication challenges into opportunities and create a stronger and more effective communication culture.

Leadership and Conflict Management

Definition and Types of Conflict

Conflicts in the business world arise from disagreements among individuals or groups with different views, values, or interests, representing a significant management challenge for organizations. In the business world, there are various types of conflicts, and these types can vary depending on the nature of the organization and its mode of operation.

Conflict of Ideas: Conflict of ideas refers to disagreements between individuals or groups within an organization who hold different opinions. Such conflicts can stem from differences in views on strategic decisions, project management, or process improvement, among other topics. A good leader addresses these conflicts constructively, bringing diverse ideas together and striving to find the best solution.

Personal Disputes: Personal disputes are conflicts based on personal relationships or incompatibilities among employees. These conflicts can arise due to personal differences, communication problems, or past disagreements. A good leader can mediate personal disputes or help team members establish positive working relationships.

Issues Related to Resource Allocation: Conflicts of this nature arise from differing opinions on how limited resources should be distributed. For example, conflicts can arise over budget allocation, allocation of personnel resources, or sharing project resources. A good leader can manage such conflicts by establishing a fair and transparent resource allocation process and explaining this process to stakeholders.

Conflicts have the potential to have negative effects on organizations, but when managed well, they can also be turned into opportunities. A good leader encourages conflicts to be handled constructively and encourages team members to think in terms of solutions. Additionally, they provide guidance for resolving conflicts using skills such as open communication, empathy, and collaboration.

Conflicts in the business world can manifest in various forms and have different underlying causes. A good leader supports organizational success by understanding the sources of conflicts and managing them effectively. Handling these conflicts constructively allows for diverse perspectives to come together, leading to better outcomes.

The Role of Leaders in Conflict Management

Conflict management plays a critical role for leaders in the business world. Leaders are responsible for effectively managing and resolving conflicts within the organization. Conflicts can arise from differences in perspectives, values, or interests. In the business world, various types of conflicts can occur, including differences of opinion, personal disputes, and issues related to resource allocation.

A good leader can identify these types of conflicts and provide guidance throughout the conflict management process. Leaders take on roles such as mediation, balancing different viewpoints, and presenting solution-oriented approaches. By facilitating communication between parties, balancing different perspectives, and addressing conflicts with a solution-focused approach, leaders ensure that conflicts lead to positive outcomes.

Furthermore, leaders reduce tension between parties by using communication and empathy skills. Empathy involves understanding the viewpoints of others and sharing the emotions they feel, and leaders use this understanding to communicate more effectively. Leaders also take on the role of developing conflict prevention and resolution strategies, promoting healthy communication within the organization, increasing collaboration, and identifying conflicts early.

Leaders lead the conflict management process, playing a critical role in maintaining organizational harmony and enhancing collaboration. Conflict management skills are essential tools for leaders to support the sustainability and success of the organization.

Effective Conflict Resolution Strategies

Effective conflict resolution strategies are essential tools that help parties involved in conflicts in organizations or the business world to increase mutual understanding, encourage collaboration, and resolve disputes. Conflicts can arise from differences in perspectives, values, or interests, and effectively managing such conflicts helps organizations maintain a healthy working environment. Here are more detailed explanations of these strategies:

Active Listening: Active listening means that a leader or conflict mediator not only hears what the parties are saying but genuinely tries to understand it. Carefully listening to the emotions, thoughts, and concerns of the parties helps them better understand how they feel and the roots of the conflict. This can build trust among the parties and keep communication open.

Building Empathy: Empathy is when a leader or mediator tries to understand the perspective of the parties and shares the emotions they are feeling. Building empathy can help parties better understand each other, strengthen emotional bonds, and encourage them to be more open with each other.

Facilitating Compromise: Compromise aims to find an acceptable middle ground between the parties. Leaders or mediators bring parties together and encourage them to balance different needs and expectations. Compromise aims to find a solution that parties can work together on and find satisfying.

Generating Creative Solutions: Creative solutions are different from traditional or conventional approaches and provide solutions that satisfy the parties involved. Leaders or mediators encourage parties to think creatively, helping them develop new and innovative approaches. This has the potential to address the root causes of conflicts and provide long-term solutions.

Leaders support parties and encourage collaboration using these conflict resolution strategies. Additionally, they aim to minimize the negative impacts of conflicts and maintain the sustainability of the organization. These strategies enable leaders to promote harmony within the organization, proactively address potential conflicts, and create a healthier work environment.

Improving Interpersonal Relationships

Mentorship and Guidance

Mentorship is a special type of relationship where an experienced professional guides and supports an individual, often with less experience or knowledge, in their professional and personal development. This relationship is widely prevalent across various industries and organizations, established with goals such as nurturing young talents, developing leadership potential, and facilitating knowledge transfer within an organization.

Mentorship fosters a strong bond between the mentor and mentee (the person receiving guidance). This bond is built on trust and typically tends to be a long-term relationship. Mentors accelerate the personal and professional development of their mentees by imparting knowledge gained from their own experiences and mistakes.

Mentorship not only facilitates knowledge transfer within the organization but also contributes to the overall success of the organization. Experienced mentors can help new employees better understand the organization's culture, values, and processes. Additionally, mentees perform more effectively by benefiting from their mentors' experiences and guidance.

Mentorship relationships hold significant value not only for professional development but also for personal growth. Mentors assist mentees in setting career goals, developing strategic plans, and working towards achieving those goals. This enables mentees to feel more motivated and navigate their careers more consciously.

Mentorship is an effective way for organizations to support young talents, cultivate their leaders, and facilitate knowledge sharing. Mentorship relationships are valuable connections where learning, growth, and personal connections converge, making them an indispensable part of the business world.

Teamwork and Collaboration

Teamwork is considered one of the cornerstones of the business world. Organizations face numerous projects and tasks where individuals with different skills, experiences, and perspectives must collaborate. This collaboration brings a host of advantages.

First and foremost, teamwork enhances productivity. A team with diverse skills tends to complete tasks more quickly and efficiently. Each member contributes expertise in their respective areas, contributing to more efficient business processes.

Furthermore, teamwork encourages creativity. Diverse perspectives and ideas allow for the emergence of new and innovative solutions. Team members learn from each other's experiences and viewpoints, which helps them solve problems more creatively.

Diversity within a team also adds significant value. Individuals with different backgrounds, cultures, and skills can help an organization serve a broader customer base and succeed in different markets. This enhances the organization's competitive advantage.

Teamwork can also boost motivation. Team members feel more motivated with the support and camaraderie that comes from working together. The sense of belonging to a team increases employees' commitment to their work.

Teamwork has a substantial impact on error reduction. Multiple sets of eyes help detect errors more quickly and prompt corrective measures.

Lastly, teamwork improves decision-making processes. Different perspectives lead to better decisions. Team members, by leveraging each other's experiences and expertise, can make more informed choices.

The role of leaders encompasses more than just bringing team members together, aligning them toward common goals, and effectively distributing tasks. A good leader channels the energy of the team, keeps team members together using communication skills, and enhances motivation.

Teamwork is a critical factor for organizational success. The amalgamation of individuals with diverse skills enables organizations to be more competitive, innovation-focused, and successful. Leaders fostering this culture significantly contribute to the long-term success of organizations.

Building Good Relationships with Colleagues

Establishing healthy and positive relationships with colleagues holds immense value in the business world. Such relationships are critical for the success and productivity of organizations. Good relationships lead to a range of positive outcomes, which contribute to the overall performance of the organization.

Firstly, good relationships lay the groundwork for collaboration. Trust and respect among colleagues promote more effective teamwork. Members of a team that trust each other tend to work better together and enhance their collaborative skills. This helps organizations complete projects faster and more effectively.

Furthermore, good relationships facilitate knowledge sharing. Open communication among colleagues speeds up the dissemination of the latest information and best practices within the organization. Knowledge sharing enables the organization to learn and grow faster.

Motivation and job satisfaction also increase as a result of good relationships.

The sense of support and camaraderie among colleagues makes employees more committed to their work and increases their motivation. A positive work environment helps employees derive more enjoyment from their jobs.

In addition, good relationships can reduce workplace stress. Stress is inevitable in the business world, but strong relationships help individuals cope with challenges. A support network among colleagues helps employees feel emotionally better and better equipped to manage stress.

Good relationships also play a crucial role in leadership and management. Effective communication and collaboration among colleagues assist leaders in working more effectively. Leaders can create a positive working environment and motivate team members.

Building good relationships with colleagues is a foundational element for organizational success. These relationships enhance collaboration, facilitate knowledge sharing, increase motivation, and reduce workplace stress. Good relationships make employees happier and more committed, contributing to the long-term sustainability of the organization.

Empathy and Understanding People's Needs

Empathy is a crucial human skill that holds great importance in the business world. This skill deepens relationships between leaders and employees and contributes positively to the success of organizations.

Empathy is particularly important for leaders because it helps them better understand and support their employees. Leaders who understand their employees' emotional states can approach them more effectively. This enables leaders to better meet the needs of their employees.

Empathy also encourages collaboration. In the business world, projects often require collaboration among people with different skills. Empathy facilitates understanding different perspectives and respecting the views of team members. This leads to more successful project completion.

Empathy also strengthens communication. Empathetic leaders can communicate more effectively with their employees because they understand their emotional states. This makes problem-solving more efficient and establishes a strong communication network among team members.

Empathy helps leaders understand their employees' needs better. Each employee is unique and has different requirements. Empathetic leaders can provide better support to their employees by understanding these differences. This helps employees perform their jobs more effectively.

Empathy is a critical skill in the business world. It helps leaders approach their employees more effectively, encourages collaboration, strengthens communication, and improves problem-solving. Empathy contributes to the success of organizations by fostering better relationships, enhancing communication, and promoting collaboration, all of which make it easier for organizations to achieve their goals.

Crisis Management and the Role of Leadership

The Importance of Crisis Management

Crisis management is an indispensable skill for organizations because unexpected events or situations can have serious consequences. Therefore, crisis management plays a critical role in preserving an organization's resilience and sustainability.

Crises can inflict financial damage. For example, natural disasters or economic fluctuations can impact an organization's revenue and lead to financial hardships. A well-defined crisis management strategy can help the organization navigate such challenges by minimizing financial risks.

However, crisis management is not limited to financial outcomes; reputation matters as well. In times of crisis, organizations need to respond with proper communication and actions. This helps in maintaining a positive public perception and safeguarding the reputation. Additionally, displaying ethical and responsible behavior enhances long-term reputation.

Crises can also threaten the survival of organizations. Particularly, major security breaches or scandals can shake the foundation of organizations. A well-thought-out crisis management plan is crucial to ensure the organization's sustainability.

Furthermore, preserving the motivation and trust of employees during crises is critical. Employees may experience worry and uncertainty, so an effective crisis management strategy focuses on supporting and informing employees.

Lastly, crises can teach organizations valuable lessons. A robust crisis management strategy allows organizations to learn from post-crisis analyses and make improvements, making them better prepared for future crises.

Crisis management is indispensable for an organization's ability to cope with potential crises. It prevents financial losses, safeguards reputation, ensures survival, motivates employees, and promotes learning from experiences.

Therefore, organizations should take crisis management strategies seriously and implement them. This enhances organizational resilience and ensures long-term success.

The Role of Leaders in Times of Crisis

The role that leaders play during crises is crucial for an organization's successful crisis management and subsequent recovery. These leaders have a significant impact from various perspectives.

First and foremost, leaders' determination and composure during crises help balance the organization's state of affairs. Their role in preventing panic and chaos and keeping things on track is paramount in preventing disruption. Leaders are known for making logical and effective decisions rather than emotional reactions during these times.

Additionally, leaders must accurately assess the magnitude of the crisis. Having quick and precise information about the source, impacts, and potential risks of the crisis is a foundational step in adopting the right strategies for the organization.

Effective communication is also a significant part of leaders' roles. Establishing clear, honest, and effective communication with both internal and external stakeholders maintains the organization's credibility and reputation. This is vital for informing employees, customers, shareholders, and the media.

Leaders must also motivate their teams and ensure collaboration during crises. This fosters a sense of solidarity among team members, helping them perform at their best even under challenging conditions. Building strong teamwork helps in overcoming crises together.

Leaders also lead the development of crisis management strategies. Crafting strategies tailored to the type of crisis and the organization's specific needs is essential for effectively managing crises.

Furthermore, leaders' roles are not limited to immediate crisis response. They must also possess the ability to manage change in the post-crisis period. Crises can create opportunities for necessary changes within organizations, and leaders can capitalize on these opportunities to make the organization stronger and more sustainable.

Leaders' roles in crisis management help organizations navigate crises successfully and move forward more robustly. Their determination, communication, motivation, strategy development, and change management abilities make them critical guides for organizations during times of crisis. Therefore, leaders making the right decisions during crises and leading their organizations is of utmost importance.

Crisis Management Strategies

Crisis management strategies are critical in determining how organizations respond and effectively overcome challenging times. These strategies prepare organizations for unexpected events and situations, and effective leadership plays a significant role in defining and implementing these strategies.

First and foremost, good leadership plans the crisis management process in advance. This involves determining the roadmap the organization will follow during a crisis. Questions like what situations are considered a crisis, who will be part of the crisis management team, how communication plans will be established, and what emergency plans will include are all essential for an organization's preparedness.

Leaders also ensure that measures are in place to keep the organization safe. By conducting risk assessments beforehand, leaders can identify potential crises and take preventive measures. Even if they cannot prevent a crisis, they can take steps to minimize damage. For example, strengthening security protocols or keeping rapid response teams ready.

Leadership during a crisis is equally important. Effective leaders are prepared to act swiftly and efficiently. They exhibit determination, expedite data and information gathering processes, and coordinate the crisis management team. Moreover, maintaining effective communication both internally and externally reduces uncertainty.

Leaders also motivate and facilitate teamwork among team members during crises. This creates a strong sense of unity among team members and enables them to perform at their best even in challenging situations. Solidarity among team members helps overcome crises together.

Leaders also play a crucial role in developing crisis management strategies. Crafting strategies tailored to the type of crisis and the organization's specific needs is essential for effectively managing crises.

Additionally, leadership's role is not confined to the immediate response to a crisis. They must possess the ability to manage change in the post-crisis period. Crises can create opportunities for necessary changes within organizations, and leaders can capitalize on these opportunities to make the organization stronger and more sustainable.

Crisis management strategies prepare organizations for crises and good leadership plays a key role in defining and implementing these strategies. Effective leadership during a crisis influences an organization's success, while leadership in the post-crisis period shapes the organization's future. Preparedness for crises and effective leadership enhance organizational resilience and contribute to long-term success.

The Future of Leadership and Human Relations in the Business World

Changing Dynamics in the Business World

The future of the business world is undergoing a significant transformation due to various factors. These factors will play a fundamental role in shaping the business world and will present new and complex challenges for leaders.

The expansion of global markets is radically changing the way business is conducted. Digital technologies and global connections provide companies with access to markets they couldn't reach before. However, this also indicates increased competition and the need to manage cultural differences.

Technological advancements are reshaping the fundamental dynamics of the business world. Artificial intelligence, automation, and big data are being used to optimize business processes and gain a competitive advantage. Leaders must keep up with these technological changes and reshape their organizations by utilizing these new tools.

Environmental sustainability is another crucial factor shaping the future of the business world. Climate change and limited natural resources are driving businesses towards more sustainable business models. Leaders should embrace environmental responsibilities and integrate these issues into their business strategies.

The evolution of workstyles is changing the structure of the business world. Remote work and flexible working hours enable employees to better balance work and personal life. Leaders need to adapt to these changing work arrangements and effectively manage their teams.

Digital transformation is rapidly occurring in every sector of the business world. Data analytics, artificial intelligence, and digital platforms enable businesses to make faster and more effective decisions. Leaders must effectively manage this digital transformation and adapt their organizations to it.

To adapt to the complexity and dynamics of the future business world, leaders must adopt a versatile approach. Factors such as the expansion of global markets, technological advancements, sustainability, changes in workstyles, and digital transformation require leaders to reassess their strategic visions and propel their organizations into the future. In this process, leaders must stand out with their flexibility, quick decision-making, and change management abilities.

The Future of Technology and Leadership

Technology is profoundly transforming the dynamics of the business world and leadership. This transformation presents both significant challenges and opportunities for businesses and leaders. Technologies such as artificial intelligence, automation, and big data analytics are particularly reshaping business processes and providing leaders with the ability to make data-driven decisions.

Artificial intelligence (AI) is making a groundbreaking impact on the business world. AI is being used in many areas, including data analysis, solving unforeseen problems, improving customer experiences, and even automating operations. Leaders need to understand how their organizations can use these technologies and adopt AI-based applications to make their processes more efficient and effective.

Automation is another important technological area used to automate repetitive tasks and business processes. Leaders should evaluate how automation can transform their operations and develop training and development strategies to align employees' skills with this new way of working.

Big data analytics provides organizations with the ability to understand and transform large amounts of data into strategic decisions. Leaders should consider how their organizations can embrace a data-focused culture and move toward turning this data into a competitive advantage.

The ability to understand and effectively use technology is a critical competitive advantage for the leaders of the future. Leaders must integrate their organizations into the digital world, strategically adopt new technologies, and adapt employees to these changes to ensure the sustainability and success of the organization.

Additionally, ethical and security issues related to these technologies should be considered. Leaders should follow best practices for data privacy, security, and ethics when using these technologies and take appropriate measures to mitigate risks.

Technology presents both opportunities and challenges for leaders. Future leaders who understand and effectively use these technologies, integrate their organizations into the digital world, and adapt employees to these changes will achieve success. In an era of rapid technological advancement, the learning and adaptation process for leaders is ongoing and provides a competitive advantage.

Sustainable Leadership and Human Relations

Sustainability has become a central focus in the business world, and leaders are increasingly expected to guide their organizations responsibly in terms of environmental and social impacts. Sustainable leadership combines long-term business success with social responsibility, and it has a profound impact in various ways.

Sustainable leadership begins with an evaluation of an organization's environmental impact. Leaders must understand the environmental impact of their processes, products, and services and develop strategies to reduce these impacts. Sustainability involves concrete actions in areas such as energy efficiency, waste reduction, and environmental certifications.

Sustainable leadership also focuses on social impacts. A good leader encourages their organization to fulfill its social responsibilities. This can take various forms, such as contributing to local communities, providing educational opportunities, or increasing workforce diversity. Additionally, it ensures that the organization operates in a way that reflects ethical values.

In terms of human relations, sustainable leadership promotes collaboration, diversity, and fairness. Leaders encourage collaboration among employees, respect different perspectives, and create an egalitarian work environment. This increases motivation, fosters creativity, and makes employees feel valued.

Sustainable leadership also supports long-term organizational success. Fulfilling environmental and social responsibilities helps organizations build a sustainable reputation. This can increase customer loyalty, create new business opportunities, and strengthen the organization's competitive advantage.

Sustainable leadership represents an approach that considers not only financial gains but also environmental and social impacts. This leadership style will become increasingly important in the future business world. By embracing sustainability principles, leaders can guide their organizations in an ethically, environmentally, and socially responsible manner.

Epilogue: Leadership and Human Relations

As I wrote this book, it was a great pleasure to convey the topics of leadership and human relations to you in the first person. Leadership and human relations are not just subjects to me; they have become a passion and a philosophy of life. This book was written with the aim of sharing this passion and knowledge with you.

Leadership is a critical factor that determines the success of an organization. However, leadership is not only a skill for those in a specific job position but also a skill that every individual can use in their daily lives. Leadership requires effective communication, empathy, and the ability to have a vision. This book aims to help you improve your leadership skills by exploring leadership around these concepts.

Human relations are essential in every aspect of life. Building good relationships, collaborating, empathizing, and understanding the needs of others are the keys to personal and professional success. This book aims to delve into the subject of human relations deeply and help you build stronger and more satisfying relationships.

The leaders of the future must have the ability to adapt to a changing world. Issues such as technology and sustainability expect leaders to generate creative and sustainable solutions. However, remember that leadership is shaped not only by strategies and plans but also by strong relationships built with people.

Thank you for reading this book. If I have been able to provide you with new perspectives on leadership and human relations, I will have achieved my goal. I wish you success on your future leadership journey and hope that you become a better leader and cultivator of human relationships by using this knowledge.

With respect,

Haktan Aydın

www.ingramcontent.com/pod-product-compliance
Lightning Source LLC
Chambersburg PA
CBHW050511290526
45786CB00007B/2521